# IT'S TIME TO LEARN ABOUT CORAL SNAKES

# It's Time to Learn about Coral Snakes

Walter the Educator

Silent King Books
A WhichHead Entertainment Imprint

Copyright © 2025 by Walter the Educator

All rights reserved. No part of this book may be reproduced in any manner whatsoever without written per- mission except in the case of brief quotations embodied in critical articles and reviews.

First Printing, 2024

Disclaimer

This book is a literary work; the story is not about specific persons, locations, situations, and/or circumstances unless mentioned in a historical context. Any resemblance to real persons, locations, situations, and/or circumstances is coincidental. This book is for entertainment and informational purposes only. The author and publisher offer this information without warranties expressed or implied. No matter the grounds, neither the author nor the publisher will be accountable for any losses, injuries, or other damages caused by the reader's use of this book. The use of this book acknowledges an understanding and acceptance of this disclaimer.

It's Time to Learn about Coral Snakes is a collectible early learning book by Walter the Educator suitable for all ages belonging to Walter the Educator's Time to Eat Book Series. Collect more books at WaltertheEducator.com

**USE THE EXTRA SPACE TO TAKE NOTES AND DOCUMENT YOUR MEMORIES**

# CORAL SNAKES

Coral snakes slither, so small and bright,

It's Time to Learn about

# Coral Snakes

With colors that warn: red, yellow, and white.

They live in warm places, both dry and wide,

And often stay hidden where they can hide.

"Red touch yellow, kill a fellow," they say,

"Red touch black, safe from attack" is the way.

This rhyme helps us tell, with a careful eye,

Which snake to watch and which one's shy.

A coral snake's bite has powerful stuff,

But they are shy and don't act tough.

They'd rather hide than bite or hiss,

So they're rarely something you'll miss.

They don't strike fast or chase you down,

They slither away without a frown.

They hunt at night and sleep all day,

So most times you won't see them play.

# It's Time to Learn about

# Coral Snakes

They eat small lizards, frogs, and more,

And wiggle through leaves upon the floor.

They use their fangs, so tiny and neat,

To catch their prey and then they eat.

Coral snakes don't have loud sound,

They won't rattle or dance around.

They're quiet, smooth, and slip through fast,

Like ribbons of color moving past.

Just give them space and step on back.

Their bright red bands are a warning sign,

To tell big animals, "This food's not fine!"

So predators leave them all alone,

And coral snakes go on their own.

There are "false" coral snakes, just for show,

With colors alike from head to toe.

But if the red and yellow touch, beware!

# It's Time to Learn about

# Coral Snakes

The true coral snake is hiding there.

They live in forests, deserts, too,

And sometimes crawl right next to you.

But don't be scared, they won't attack,

So now you know, if you see bold stripes,

Learn the rhyme and avoid the types.

Respect the wild and keep it cool

# It's Time to Learn about

# Coral Snakes

That's how we stay safe, like nature's rule!

# ABOUT THE CREATOR

Walter the Educator is one of the pseudonyms for Walter Anderson. Formally educated in Chemistry, Business, and Education, he is an educator, an author, a diverse entrepreneur, and he is the son of a disabled war veteran. "Walter the Educator" shares his time between educating and creating. He holds interests and owns several creative projects that entertain, enlighten, enhance, and educate, hoping to inspire and motivate you. Follow, find new works, and stay up to date with Walter the Educator™

**at WaltertheEducator.com**

www.ingramcontent.com/pod-product-compliance
Lightning Source LLC
LaVergne TN
LVHW051920060526
838201LV00060B/4097